BEAUTIFUL DOODLING

STERLING CHILDREN'S BOOKS
New York

STERLING CHILDREN'S BOOKS
New York

An Imprint of Sterling Publishing
1166 Avenue of the Americas
New York, NY 10036

STERLING CHILDREN'S BOOKS and the distinctive Sterling
Children's Books logo are trademarks of Sterling Publishing Co., Inc.

First Sterling edition published in 2016.

First published in Great Britain in 2015 by Buster Books, an imprint of Michael O'Mara Books Limited,
9 Lion Yard, Tremadoc Road, London SW4 &NQ

© 2015 by Buster Books

Illustrations by Cindy Wilde, edited by Imogen Williams, designed by Zoe Bradley
Cover designed by Angie Allison

ISBN 978-1-4549-1882-0

Distributed in Canada by Sterling Publishing
c/o Canadian Manda Group, 664 Annette Street, Toronto, Ontario, Canada M6S 2C8

For information about custom editions, special sales, and premium and corporate purchases, please
contact Sterling Special Sales at 800-805-5489 or specialsales@sterlingpublishing.com.

Manufactured in China

Lot #:
2 4 6 8 10 9 7 5 3 1
09/15

www.sterlingpublishing.com/kids

Contents

Introduction

Use this book to learn how to draw beautiful pictures. Each drawing project has six step-by-step instructions, including a feature pattern, to help you illustrate.

Create your own picture in the empty frames at the end of the instructions. The first step of each project is lightly drawn already to help you get started. At the end of each project is a finished drawing for you to color in.

Learn to draw wonderful feathery birds like a peacock in the Beautiful Birds section, or illustrate underwater creatures in Under the Sea. Get outdoorsy in the Nature Trail section and learn to draw everything from elephants to rabbits in Amazing Animals. Practice beautiful designs in the Pretty Patterns section, draw delicious treats in Fancy Food, and doodle gorgeous patterns in Decorative Designs.

Beautiful Doodling will help you create your own enchanting world.

Robin

Decorate the robin's wing with this beautiful flower.

Flower Pattern

Draw a big circle with a smaller circle inside it.

Add petal shapes with three short lines inside them.

Draw a curved line around the edge and a design in the middle with dots in it.

Practice the pattern here.

Beautiful Birds

1. Draw the rounded outline of your robin using curved and sweeping lines.

2. Give your robin a tail, using a slightly curved rectangle. Then draw a large teardrop shape for its wing on the left-hand side and a large semicircle for your robin's breast on the right-hand side.

3. Using simple lines add in two legs, a big gleaming eye, and a beak. You can also show your robin's head by drawing a curved line behind its eye joining up with the top of the wing.

4. Add the flower pattern to your robin's wing and draw a feather pattern in the section underneath its wing using overlapping petal shapes.

5. Add some smaller petal shapes and lines inside the feather pattern and around your robin's head. You can also add a pretty heart border around your robin's breast.

6. For the finishing touches, draw some dashed lines and V-shaped lines and dots in the empty spaces to create different feathery effects.

Draw your robin in this frame.

Color me in.

Rooster

Learn to draw a decorative feather pattern to doodle on your rooster.

Scallop Pattern

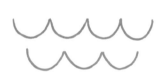

Draw two scalloped lines, one underneath the other.

Add semicircles between each scallop shape.

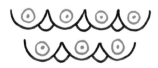

Draw a small circle in each scallop shape, and add a dot in the middle.

Practice the pattern here.

Beautiful Birds

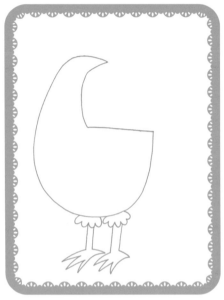

1. Draw a straight line for the back and a sweeping curved line down for the tummy and up to the head. Draw two legs with cloud shapes at the top and triangle shapes for the feet.

2. Draw a teardrop shape on the body for the wing. Then use a cloud shape to draw the crest on its head and add a teardrop shape on the chin. Use curved lines to draw curly feathers for the tail.

3. Draw swirly lines in the crest, under the chin and between the feathers of the tail. Give your rooster a gleaming eye and a beak. Draw small lines on the legs and feet for shadows.

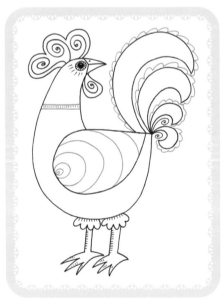

4. Draw scalloped lines around the edges of the tail feathers, and add a stripe around the neck. Draw little vertical lines inside the stripe around the neck and big curved lines in the wing.

5. Decorate your rooster's neck with the scallop pattern. Then draw petal shapes and lines in each section of the wing.

6. To complete your rooster, draw a loopy line and dots around the neck. Add small scalloped lines on the wing, fill the tail feathers with petal shapes and lines, and add dots on its body.

Draw your rooster in this frame.

Color me in.

Peacock

This feathery design will make your peacock look even more fantastic.

Feather Pattern

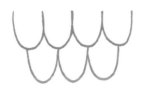

Draw a row of petal shapes with a shorter row underneath.

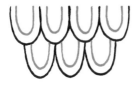

Add a smaller petal shape inside the bigger petals.

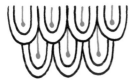

Finish by adding a line with a dot at the end inside each smaller petal shape.

Practice the pattern here.

1. Draw a vase shape with a circle behind it for the body of your peacock and a giant leaf shape for the tail. Add two long triangles for legs, including small lines for the feet.

2. Add a small fan shape to create the crest and give your peacock an eye. Draw some stripes on its legs and also add a beak.

3. Divide the tail into nine vertical sections. Then add a row of little semicircles around the bottom part of your peacock's tail. Inside each of the nine sections of the tail, draw a balloon shape on a string.

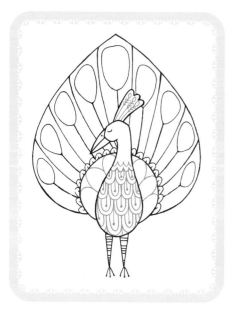

4. Next, draw two scalloped lines on the neck. Add the feather pattern on the body underneath. Include feathery line detail inside the crest and semicircles in the circular body of your peacock.

5. Now add more detail to the tail by drawing two smaller loops inside each balloon shape and small bows along the lines.

6. Add lines around the outside layer of the balloon shapes in the top of the tail. Finally, draw leaf-like patterns in the semicircles on the body of your peacock and decorate with dots.

Draw your peacock in this frame.

Beautiful Birds

Color me in.

Feathers

Use zigzag patterns to decorate empty spaces on your feathers.

Zigzag Pattern

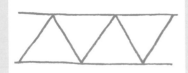

Draw two horizontal lines with a zigzag line in the middle.

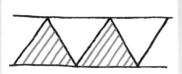

Add diagonal parallel lines inside the bottom triangles.

Then draw parallel lines going in the opposite direction in the top triangles.

Practice the pattern here.

1. To create the quill, draw long stem shapes. At the end of the quills, draw a curved rectangle shape and four smaller rectangle shapes.

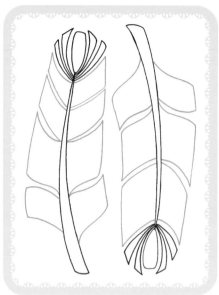

2. Use curved lines to draw big sections on each side of the quills.

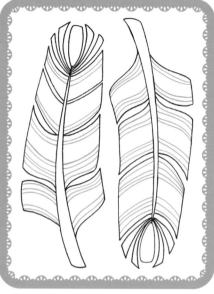

3. Draw parallel lines at the top and bottom of each section.

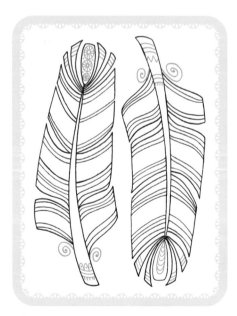

4. Decorate the top and bottom of each feather using swirls, circles, semicircles, dots, and lines.

5. Use a mixture of the zigzag pattern and other patterns to fill in the empty sections of your feathers. You can use zigzags, ovals, and semicircles.

6. Finish off your feathers by adding in detail to the remaining sections, like short lines, triangles, dots, and circles.

Draw your feathers in this frame.

BEAUTIFUL BIRDS

Color me in.

Crab

Doodle crazy splotches to camouflage your crab.

Splotch Pattern

Use a curvy line to draw a splotch.

Fill the splotch with dots.

Practice the pattern here.

1. Create the body of your crab by drawing a squashed diamond shape and add a scalloped line across the top.

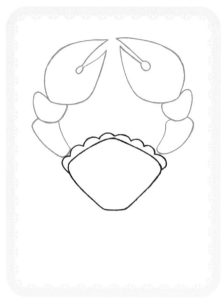

2. Draw the two front claws by making rounded shapes coming from the body of the crab. Include two giant pincers on the end.

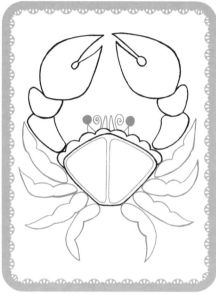

3. Add in eight finger shapes for the legs and draw two triangles inside your crab's body. Give your crab two bulging eyes and some antennae.

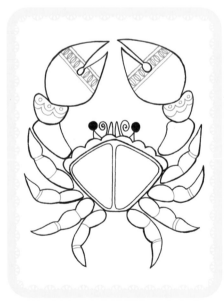

4. Divide each of the legs into sections. Add a scalloped line on the claws. On the pincers, draw four parallel lines with little circles between them across the middle.

5. Add parallel lines to the tips of the pincers, legs, and the scalloped edge around the top of the body.

6. Finally, decorate the empty spaces with the splotch pattern.

Draw your crab in this frame.

Color me in.

Fish

Use this swirly scale pattern to decorate your fish.

Scale Pattern

Draw a row of petal shapes with a shorter row next to it.

Add smaller petal shapes with a swirl inside each big petal.

Practice the pattern here.

1. For the big fish, draw a circular shape with two small bumps for the lips. Add a tail and a head. For the smaller fish, draw a teardrop shape and give it a tail and a face.

2. Give both fish a big eye and draw another line on the inside of the tails and around the faces. Then add lots of petal shapes along the top and bottom of your fish to create fins.

3. Draw semicircles around the edge of their faces and fill them with short lines. Use curved lines to divide their tails into sections and add a loopy pattern and dots at the end of each tail.

4. Add the scale pattern to the bodies of both fish.

5. Draw a loopy line around the eyes and decorate the stripes behind the faces with circles and scalloped lines. Decorate with dots.

6. Complete your fish by doodling patterns on the fins, such as swirls or curved lines. Use curved lines and dots in different sections of the tail.

Draw your fish in this frame.

Color me in.

Seahorse

Make your seahorse stunning with this beautiful swirly design.

Swirl Pattern

Draw a line with two semicircles over the top.

Add three swirls inside the smaller semicircle.

To finish, add a row of swirls inside the bigger semicircle.

Practice the pattern here.

1. Draw a straight line for the back with a curl at the bottom. Then draw up toward the head creating a bump for the chest at the top. Use curved lines to draw the head and straighter lines to draw a long nose.

2. Give your seahorse an eye and draw a rectangle shape on its back. Add long lines down the back with small teardrop shapes at the end. Add four more to the front.

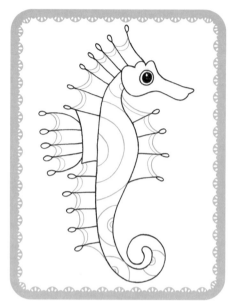

3. Draw two curved lines between each long line, joining them up to create fins. Add big curved lines on your seahorse's body to divide it into sections.

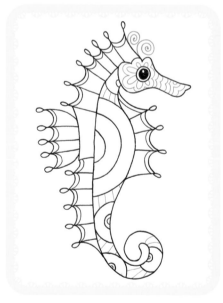

4. Draw two spirals on top of your seahorse's head. Add small curved lines to decorate some sections of the body and head.

5. Inside each fin, draw small sausage shapes.

6. Finally, use the swirl pattern to fill in the remaining sections on your seahorse's body.

Draw your seahorse in this frame.

Color me in.

Shells

Use this pretty pattern to decorate your shells.

Shell Pattern

Draw two horizontal lines with semicircles in between them.

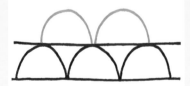

Add more semicircles along the top.

Use curved lines to divide each semicircle into four segments and draw dots between each one.

Practice the pattern here.

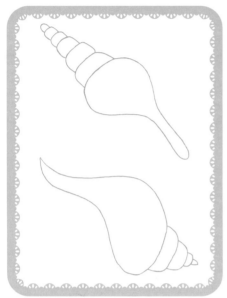

1. Use curved lines to draw two big teardrop shapes for the base of your shells. Create a spiral effect on top by adding curved rectangle shapes getting smaller and smaller.

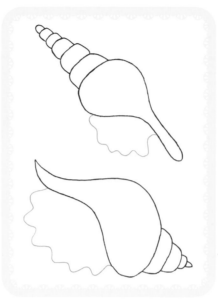

2. Add a wavy line in a wide arc around the bottom of each shell.

3. Draw a teardrop shape inside the bottom of each shell and divide the base of the shell into four segments using curved lines.

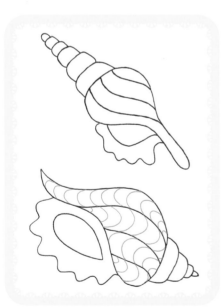

4. In the bottom shell, use wavy lines to decorate each segment.

5. In the top shell, use lots of teardrop shapes to decorate the base and the spiral of the shell.

6. To finish off your shells, add the shell pattern around the bottom of the shells and around the spiral of the bottom shell.

Draw your shells in this frame.

Color me in.

Sun

This curvy pattern will give your sun beaming rays.

Sun Ray Pattern

Draw two curved lines with pointy petal shapes inside.

Divide the front petals into segments using curved lines.

Add swirls inside the back petals.

Practice the pattern here.

1. Draw one big circle with a smaller circle inside it.

2. Fill in the space between the two circles with the sun ray pattern to create rays.

3. Draw a rectangle shape in the smaller circle to create a nose and extend the top lines outward so they join the edge of the circle. Add a second curved line to create eyebrows.

4. Give your sun beaming eyes using semicircles, and use curved lines to give your sun lips and nostrils.

5. Draw small circles between each sun ray. Then add a semicircle at the bottom of your sun's face to give it a chin. Add two circles for cheeks with triangle shapes around the edge so they look like small suns.

6. Finish your sun by adorning its face with circles around the eyes and teardrop shapes and circles on its forehead. Add curved lines over the eyes and straight lines underneath them.

Draw your sun in this frame.

Color me in.

Beetle

Doodle this spotty pattern all over your beetle to give it a shiny effect.

Spot Pattern

Draw two circular shapes.

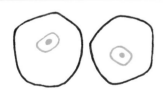

Add a dot in the middle with a circle around it.

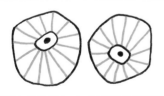

Use straight lines to connect the bigger circles to the smaller circles.

Practice the pattern here.

1. Create your beetle's body by drawing one big petal shape for the bottom half and an oval shape for the top half.

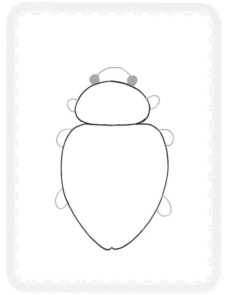

2. Add six semicircles around the edge of the body. Draw two big dots for eyes and use a curved line to join the eyes together, creating the head.

3. Use roof-tile shapes to draw your beetle's legs. At the end of each leg draw two small swirly lines.

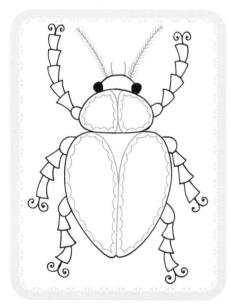

4. Draw two small lines and two big lines on your beetle's head for antennae. Divide the top half of your beetle into two and do the same for the bottom half. Then draw scalloped lines inside each section.

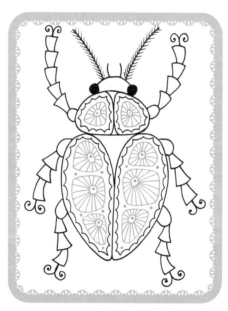

5. Add the spot pattern to the middle sections of your beetle's body and decorate with dots.

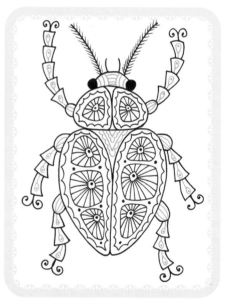

6. Finish by adding decorative patterns and curved lines to fill in the blank spaces on the head and in the legs.

Draw your beetle in this frame.

Color me in.

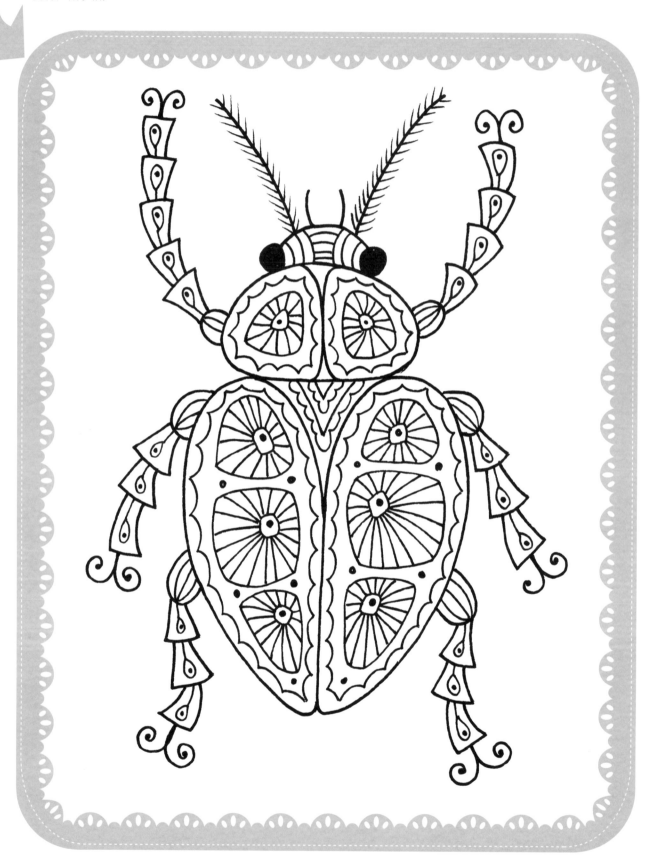

Flower

Learn to draw this swirly leaf pattern and use it to decorate your fantastic flower.

Leaf Pattern

Draw a curved line with a dot at the top.

Add six swirls coming out from the stalk.

Use a scalloped line to draw around the edge of the stalk and swirls to make a leaf shape.

Practice the pattern here.

1. Start your flower by drawing the stalk, with a small semicircle at the top for the bud. Then draw two curving petals with curls at each end.

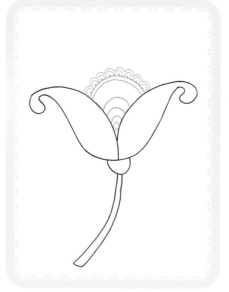

2. Now draw semicircles between the two big petals. Start small and get bigger. When you reach halfway up the petals, draw a scalloped border along the top.

3. Draw a leaf on each side of the stalk and three petals with pointy tops across the top of your flower. Add another line inside the petals and leaves.

4. Add in the leaf pattern on the leaves and big petals. Draw a double scalloped line inside the petals.

5. Add stripes on the stalk and bud. Decorate each layer of the middle of your flower with different patterns, using circles, dots, and oval shapes. Draw three small balloon shapes in each petal.

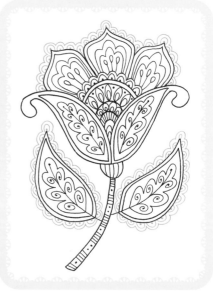

6. To complete your flower, draw a scalloped border around the edge of the leaves and petals. Decorate with semicircles and dots.

Draw your flower in this frame.

Color me in.

Frog

These star shapes will brighten up your frog.

Star Pattern

Draw a swirl and then add triangles around the edge.

Add three straight lines between each triangle.

Draw a scalloped line in a circle around the edge and add dots in the indents and in the triangles.

Practice the pattern here.

1. Draw the body and head of your frog using an oval shape for the body and a squashed heart shape with a curved middle for the head.

2. Add two back legs made up of leaf shapes with three lollipop-shaped toes at the end of each leg.

3. Give your frog a face by drawing one curved line across the bottom of the head for its mouth. Add two dashed lines for the nostrils and two gleaming eyes.

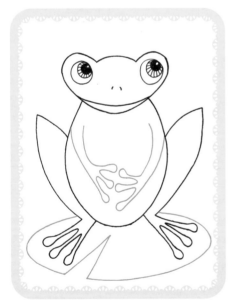

4. Draw two front legs using curved lines with three lollipop-shaped fingers. Add a lily pad for your frog to sit on, using a circle shape with a triangle taken out of it.

5. Add curved lines between the fingers and toes to create a webbed effect. Also add curved lines by the knees. Divide your lily pad into segments using straight lines and draw a scalloped line around the edge.

6. Finally, add the star pattern to your frog. To make the star pattern larger, add extra layers around the edge. Add small circles in any empty spaces.

Draw your frog in this frame.

Color me in.

Butterfly

These decorative dots will make your butterfly look even more beautiful.

Dot Pattern

Draw a circle with short lines around the edge.

Add a diamond shape with a circle in the middle.

Repeat these steps in the middle of the small circle and add dots to decorate.

Practice the pattern here.

1. Draw an oval and two teardrop shapes for your butterfly's body and head. Add two large triangle shapes for the top wings, and use a scalloped line to draw the bottom wings.

2. Use curved lines to draw triangle shapes on the top wings and teardrop shapes on the bottom wings. Give your butterfly eyes and antennae. Divide the body and head into segments using stripes.

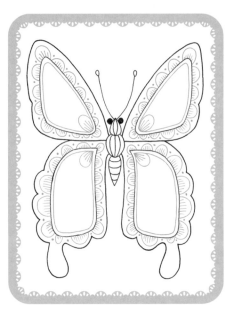

3. Draw a second line inside the wing segments. Add semicircles around the edges of the wings and fill them with short lines. Draw the same petal shape in the corner of each wing segment. Decorate with dots.

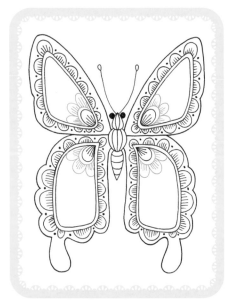

4. Draw three of the same petal shapes in the corners of each wing segment.

5. Add the dot pattern into the corners of each wing segment and on the small loops at the bottom.

6. Complete your butterfly by drawing a scalloped line around the petal shapes in the wings. Then add teardrop shapes in the empty spaces on the wings.

Draw your butterfly in this frame.

Color me in.

Lion

Use this wavy design to give your lion a massive mane.

Wavy Pattern

Draw a scalloped line and a curved line. Connect them.

Add curved lines inside every other segment.

To finish, draw curved lines going in the opposite direction in the empty segments.

Practice the pattern here.

1. Use curved lines to draw the face of your lion and surround it with a big circular scalloped line. Draw two curved lines coming down for the body.

2. Add two triangular ears above the face, a straight line down the front of the body, and two petal shapes for the back legs. Then add four semicircle shapes for the feet.

3. Draw a triangle nose with a smiling mouth and some hairy eyebrows. Then divide the ears into two halves using a curved line and color the nose in.

4. Give your lion two eyes by using lots of semicircles and short lines. Add a tail and some whiskers. Draw short lines inside the bottom half of its ears.

5. Add the wavy pattern inside your lion's mane.

6. To finish off, draw some pretty petal patterns on the legs, give your lion toenails, and use curved lines to divide the bushy tail into little segments.

Draw your lion in this frame.

Color me in.

Rabbit

This swirly flower pattern will make your rabbit look perfect for spring.

Teardrop Pattern

Start by drawing a swirl.

Add teardrop shapes around the edge of the swirl.

Inside each teardrop shape, draw a smaller teardrop.

Practice the pattern here.

1. Start by drawing the outline of your rabbit. Use leaf shapes to create big ears, an oval shape for the head, and a sweeping, curved line for the body.

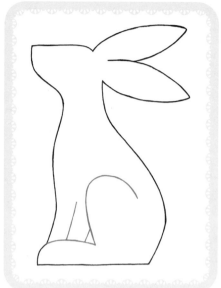

2. Now add two big curved lines to create the hind leg of your rabbit. Draw two straight lines for the front legs.

3. Give your rabbit a big fluffy tail, a face, and some whiskers. Also draw a smaller leaf shape inside the bottom ear and draw a stripe around its neck.

4. Decorate your rabbit with the teardrop pattern.

5. Add a few more simple flowers to your rabbit's ears and legs.

6. Finally, decorate your rabbit's collar with little spirals and fill in any empty spaces with small circles and hearts.

Draw your rabbit in this frame.

Color me in.

Fox

Use this pretty splash design to decorate your fox.

Splash Pattern

Draw seven teardrop shapes in a row like a splash.

Then add a smaller teardrop shape inside each one.

Practice the pattern here.

Amazing Animals

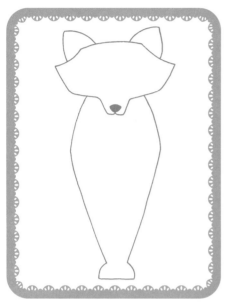

1. Start by drawing a vase shape for your fox's body, with rounded feet at the bottom. Then draw the head using curved lines, and add a nose and two triangular ears.

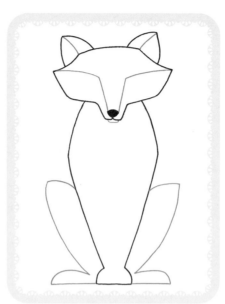

2. Use leaf shapes to draw the back legs and feet. Then divide each ear into two sections. Draw straight lines from your fox's cheeks in toward the eye and then down to the nose. Add a mouth.

3. Draw curving zigzag lines across the chest for a furry effect. Add triangles on the side of your fox's cheeks and give it slanted eyes. Draw a straight line down the middle of your fox and draw lines for toes.

4. Draw petal and heart shapes on your fox's knees, forehead, and on each side of the furry chest.

5. Use the splash pattern to decorate the legs. Add a striped band above the nose and use circles, swirls, and zigzag lines to complete your fox's face.

6. Use straight lines to draw six long whiskers. Finally, add short lines in the ears, around the bottom of the legs, and on the furry chest.

Draw your fox in this frame.

Color me in.

Elephant

Decorate your elephant with this pretty paisley pattern.

Paisley Pattern

Draw a teardrop shape.

Add two smaller teardrops inside it.

Decorate the edges of the teardrops with semicircles and a circle at the end.

Practice the pattern here.

1. Draw an oval shape for your elephant's head, then draw an L-shape for the trunk.

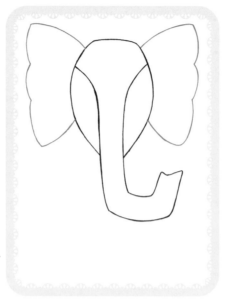

2. Give your elephant ears by drawing two big fan shapes on either side of its head.

3. Use curved lines for the body and legs. Add eyes, short lines on its head for hair, and fan shapes in the ears.

4. Give your elephant tusks and a tail and decorate with small lines. Use semicircles to give your elephant toenails. Draw stripes on each leg and V-shaped lines on its forehead.

5. Add the paisley pattern inside the ears. Decorate your elephant with pretty patterns, such as flowers around the eyes, scalloped lines, circles, dots, and teardrop shapes. Draw a tassle hanging on its forehead.

6. Complete your elephant by adding hearts, dots, and little star shapes in the empty spaces. Decorate the trunk with a leaf pattern and teardrop shapes.

Draw your elephant in this frame.

Color me in.

Stag

This swirly leaf design will make your stag look magnificent.

Laurel Pattern

Draw a long curved line with a smaller curved line coming off from the side.

Draw small leaf shapes all the way along each line.

Practice the pattern here.

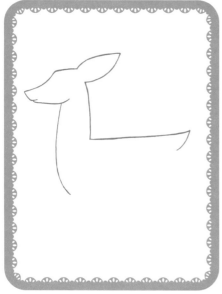

1. Draw the top half of your stag, with two straight lines for the neck and back. Draw a leaf shape for the ear and rounded lines for the head and front of the neck.

2. Now add in the bottom half of your stag by using two long rectangles for a front and back leg. Use a curved line between the tail and back leg.

3. Give your stag another ear using the same leaf shape. Use the same rectangle shapes to add two more legs.

4. Draw a smaller leaf shape inside your stag's front ear. Color in its nose and give it an eye. Color in its hooves, and then draw two big antlers using wiggly lines.

5. Add in the laurel pattern to decorate your stag's body.

6. Finish off your stag with little circles on the antlers and legs. Draw two parallel lines above each hoof. Finally, use a curved line with a spiral at the end to give your stag an eyebrow.

Draw your stag in this frame.

Color me in.

Horse

Use this petal-shaped pattern to give your horse pretty detail.

Petal Pattern

Draw a line with semicircles going in different directions.

Keep adding layers of semicircles on top of the first layer.

Then draw around the edge with one big scalloped line.

Practice the pattern here.

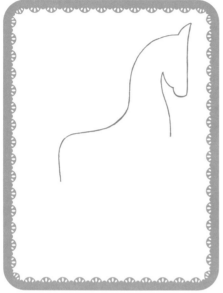

1. Draw a big sweeping curved line for your horse's back and neck. Add a small triangle shape for the ear and a vertical line for the front of the head. Draw a chin and cheek and then add a curved line for the neck.

2. Still using curved lines, add a back leg using a rectangle shape and a bent front leg.

3. Draw another front and back leg just behind the ones described in step two. Add a tail and draw a curly mane, using lots of connected swirls. Add a scalloped line around the swirls.

4. Draw connected leaf shapes for the carousel pole. Use semicircles for a saddle and decorate the edge with small circles. Add curved lines for the straps, saddle, and hooves. Give your horse an eye.

5. Use the petal pattern to decorate your horse's body.

6. Add some final decorative designs using a flowery pattern in the saddle, swirls in the straps, and teardrop shapes on your horse's body.

Draw your horse in this frame.

Color me in.

Lantern

Decorate your lantern with this crisscross pattern.

Crisscross Pattern

Draw a row of diamond shapes.

Add a dot inside each diamond.

Use curved lines to join each diamond at the top and bottom.

Practice the pattern here.

PRETTY PATTERNS

1. Draw a square shape for the box with a long rectangle across the top. Add a pointed dome shape on top.

2. Draw a double line around the inside of the box and the inside of the dome. Add a circle and ring shape at the very top.

3. Add the crisscross pattern down each side and across the top of the lantern. Then draw half the pattern around the edge of the dome shape.

4. Decorate the corners of the square and the dome with small hearts. Add dots and circles across the top and bottom of the box.

5. Draw more hearts all over the inside of the box and dome, but leave some white spaces.

6. Fill in the remaining white spaces with circles and teardrop shapes.

Draw your lantern in this frame.

Color me in.

Russian Doll

Use this lovely loopy design to decorate your doll's clothes.

Loopy Pattern

Draw a loopy line with dots in between each loop.

Draw exactly the same shape as step one, but upside down.

Add a scalloped line around the edge of the loopy lines and draw a short line coming out of each indent.

Practice the pattern here.

1. Draw a vase shape for the body of your doll, with a circle at the top for the face and two small teardrop shapes under the circle for a bow.

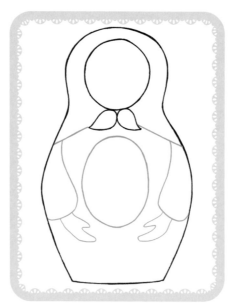

2. Next, draw straight lines out from the corners of the bow to the edges of your doll. Use curved lines to draw the sleeves and hands. Add an oval to the middle of your doll's body.

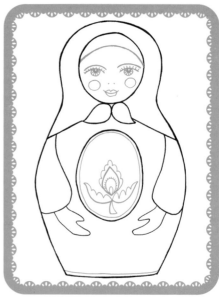

3. Start to decorate inside the oval shape by drawing another smaller oval inside. Then start to draw the stalk, leaves, and bud of a small flower using curved and scalloped lines. Add features to your doll's face.

4. Use spiral lines to give your doll hair and draw a scalloped line around the top edge of the head. Finish the flower in the central oval by using scalloped lines to create larger petals.

5. Draw the loopy pattern around the sleeves, neck, oval, and bottom of the body to decorate your doll.

6. Finally, use circles and hearts to fill in the bow and around the head of your doll.

Draw your Russian doll in this frame.

Color me in.

Star

Learn to draw this detailed design to make your star look spectacular.

Delicate Pattern

Draw two swirls with a pointy petal shape on top.

Use curved lines to draw a dome shape inside it.

Then draw semicircle shapes around the edge and a petal shape in the middle.

Practice the pattern here.

Pretty Patterns

1. Draw a hexagon with curved lines. Then use scalloped lines to draw around the edge of the hexagon, with larger semicircles over each point.

2. Add six petal shapes around each point of the hexagon. Then repeat step one and draw a smaller version inside the hexagon. Add semicircles in the inside corners of the big hexagon.

3. Draw two big swirls and two small swirls between each petal shape. Add part of the delicate pattern in the petal shapes.

4. Add the rest of the delicate pattern between each pair of swirls.

5. Add another layer of the delicate pattern on the end of a line coming from the points of the petals.

6. Draw an outline around the whole star, adding small loops at the tip of each point.

Draw your star in this frame.

Color me in.

Dog

These swirly dots will make your spotty dog look superb.

Spiral Pattern

Draw a square spiral shape.

Add a scalloped line around the edge.

Draw a dot inside each indent of the scalloped line.

Practice the pattern here.

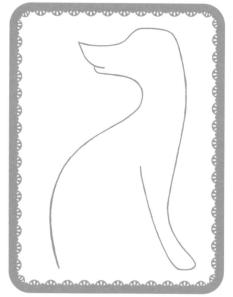

1. Draw the outline of your dog using curved lines. Create a front leg using a rectangle shape and a nose by using a pointed triangle shape.

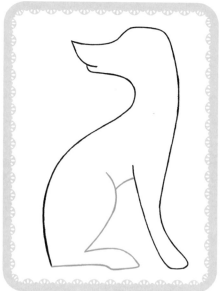

2. Give your dog a back leg by using curved lines and use a straight line to join its paw up to its body.

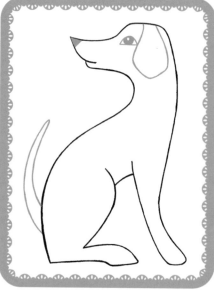

3. Add a tail using curved lines and a big ear using a teardrop shape. Draw a nose and an eye.

4. Add dots to your dog's nose and draw a decorative collar using zigzag lines.

5. Now use the spiral pattern to give your dog swirly spots all over its body and ear.

6. Finally, draw some stripes inside the zigzag collar. Draw small circles to fill the empty spaces on the dog's body. Add a decorative scalloped line and dots above the collar.

Draw your dog in this frame.

Color me in.

Fans

Draw these pretty flower patterns on your fans to make them beautiful.

Floral Pattern

Draw three small balloon shapes on curved lines.

Add a cloud shape around the top.

Draw two small leaf shapes on each side of the stalks.

Practice the pattern here.

97

Pretty Patterns

1. Create the outline of your fans by drawing a triangle with a long, curved edge. Draw a small triangle at the point of each fan and add a smaller curved line inside the bottom of both fans.

2. Add another curved line along the top of your fans. Draw triangular stripes in the bottom section of your fans and give the curved line a scalloped edge.

3. Connect the semicircles with smaller semicircles and then draw a scalloped line over the top.

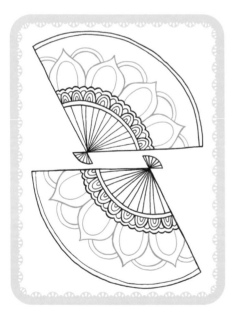

4. Now draw four pointed petal shapes in each fan. Inside each petal shape, add a semicircle. Then connect the petals with curved rings.

5. Add the floral pattern to each petal. Then add the top of the floral pattern in the semicircles behind. Draw short curved lines between the tops of each petal.

6. Finally, fill in the curved rings with little stripes and draw a scalloped pattern with dots around the top of each fan.

Draw your fans in this frame.

Color me in.

Cupcake

Decorate your cupcake with this heart-shaped design to make it look even more delicious.

Heart Pattern

Draw a rectangle with two hearts inside it.

Add a smaller heart inside and a bigger heart outside each one.

Keep drawing heart shapes around the outside until you fill the space in the rectangle.

Practice the pattern here.

1. For the cupcake paper, draw a curved box with a scalloped line across the top. Add the frosting with curved lines, to make three sausage shapes. Draw a scalloped line across the bottom of the frosting.

2. Draw a stripe across the top of the cupcake paper. Divide each section of frosting into four segments using curved lines.

3. Inside the stripe at the top of the cupcake paper, draw small vertical lines and add semicircles along the edge. Add more curved segments inside the bottom section of the frosting.

4. Now add the heart pattern inside the cupcake paper.

5. Cover your cake and frosting with small circles and hearts.

6. Add two butterflies on sticks to the top of your cake using two oval shapes for the body and four teardrop shapes for the wings. Decorate the wings and give the butterflies antennae.

Draw your cupcake in this frame.

Fancy Food

Color me in.

Ice Cream

This diamond crisscross pattern is perfect for your ice cream cone.

Waffle Pattern

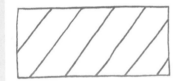

Draw a rectangle and then draw diagonal lines inside it.

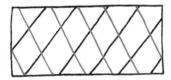

Then add diagonal lines going in the other direction.

Inside each diamond shape, draw a smaller diamond shape.

Practice the pattern here.

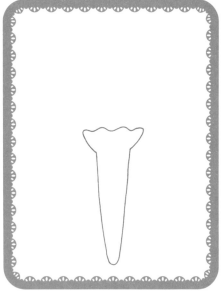

1. Draw a sausage shape for the cone of your ice cream and add a wavy line along the top.

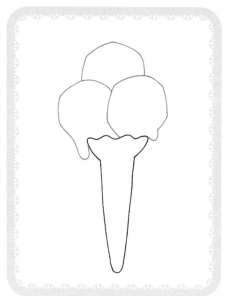

2. Add three scoops of ice cream and use curved loops at the bottom to create a dripping effect.

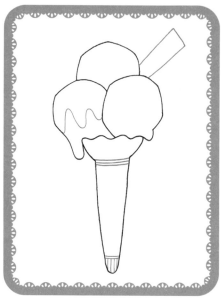

3. Draw stripes around the top and bottom of the cone. Use a rectangle shape to draw a chocolate straw coming from the top of the ice cream. Add a wavy line across the middle of the ice cream scoop on the left.

4. Complete the chocolate straw by filling it with wiggly stripes. Add the waffle pattern to the long section of the cone and a scalloped line across the top.

5. Add dots to the bottom section of the left ice cream scoop. Create a swirly effect by drawing wavy lines in the ball next to it.

6. Use small circles and rectangles to draw sprinkles on top of your ice cream. Add three hearts in the top of the cone. Finish by adding small circles and swirls around the outside of your ice cream.

Draw your ice cream in this frame.

Fancy Food

Color me in.

Gingerbread House

Use this swirly line to make your gingerbread house look absolutely scrumptious.

Shell Pattern

Draw swirls in a connected row.

Connect the bottom of the swirls with curved lines.

Then do the same to connect the swirls along the top.

Practice the pattern here.

1. On top of a horizontal line draw a simple house shape, with the walls and roof curving inward. Decorate the bottom edge of the roof with a scalloped line.

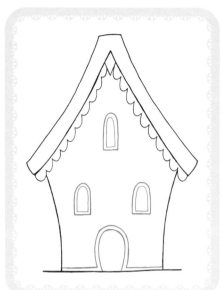

2. Add three windows and a front door using semicircle shapes. Draw round each semicircle shape again.

3. Add a chimney made up of rectangular blocks and give the front door a letterbox and door handle. Give each window a pair of shutters and draw diamond shapes inside the bottom windows to create curtains.

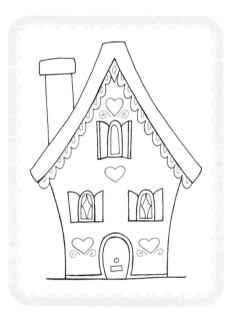

4. Decorate your house with hearts and swirls, and add small semicircles to the scalloped line under the roof. Add a small diamond shape at the point of the roof.

5. Add the shell pattern inside the roof, along the middle of the house, and along the bottom of the front door.

6. Draw bricks on the chimney using squares and rectangles, and add dots in the bottom-right corner of each brick. Finish by doodling teardrop patterns in the blank spaces.

Draw your gingerbread house in this frame.

Color me in.

Steam Train

This swirly steam pattern will make your train look stunning.

Twirly Pattern

Draw swirls in a row, gradually getting larger.

Add a second line along the top and bottom.

Repeat step two.

Practice the pattern here.

Decorative Designs

1. Create a simple train shape by drawing one big circle and three smaller circles for wheels. On top of the wheels, add a square for the front of the train and a rectangle for the cabin.

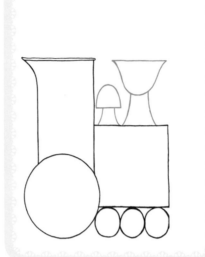

2. For the small chimney, draw a mushroom shape on top of two curved lines. For the bigger chimney, draw another mushroom but with an upside-down top.

3. Draw a triangular shape at the front of your train, and a headlight using two swirls and a thin rectangle. Add the steam using the steam pattern.

4. Add a door with a window on the cabin. Draw some decorative stripes on the chimney and on the front of the train. Include circles inside all the wheels. Divide the triangle at the front of the train into three sections using curved lines.

5. Draw small circles and dots on the train, wheels, chimneys, and headlight.

6. Decorate the empty spaces with petal patterns, hearts, and swirls.

Draw your steam train in this frame.

Color me in.

Windmill

Decorate the sails of your wonderful windmill with this detailed design. Draw this in pencil first so you can rub out overlapping lines.

Circle Pattern

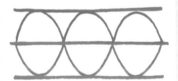

Draw three horizontal lines with oval shapes inside.

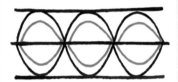

Add a circle shape inside each oval.

Draw a smaller oval in the middle and add triangles between each larger oval.

Practice the pattern here.

1. Using a pencil, draw straight lines for the walls and floor of your windmill and curved lines for the dome roof.

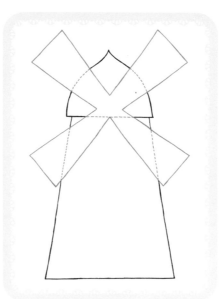

2. Draw the sail on to the front of your windmill. The lines will overlap the windmill building you drew in step one. Erase the overlapping lines.

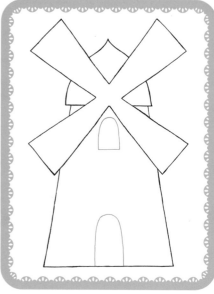

3. Add a front door and a window, using curved lines.

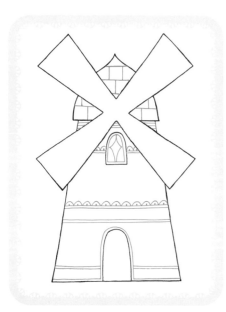

4. Draw parallel lines across your windmill and decorate with scalloped lines. Use straight lines to draw bricks on the roof and give the window curtains using a diamond shape.

5. Use the circle pattern on the sails, the front door, and along the stripes on the windmill.

6. Finally, draw flower shapes in the empty spaces on your windmill.

Draw your windmill in this frame.

Color me in.

Pretty Towers

Use this flowery pattern to decorate your magnificent towers.

Stem Pattern

Draw a horizontal line with a row of vertical lines on top of it.

Add three teardrop shapes between each vertical line.

Draw a smaller teardrop shape inside each big one.

Practice the pattern here.

Decorative Designs

1. Draw three big teardrop shapes for the roofs of the towers. Then draw two straight lines coming down from each roof to create the walls.

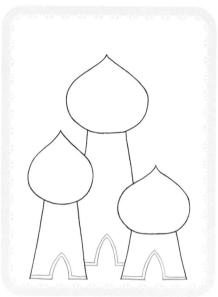

2. Along the bottom of each tower, draw a double line with an arch shape in the middle to create doorways.

3. Color in the doors. Then add small windows to each tower. Draw circles on top of the point of each roof and use petal shapes and swirly lines to create spires at the very top.

4. Draw stripes across the towers, roofs, and in the balls on top of each building.

5. Use a mixture of the stem pattern and other designs to decorate sections of the roofs. Use swirls, circles, curved lines, and petal shapes.

6. Finish your pretty towers by decorating the remaining spaces with swirls, dots, lines, and semicircles.

Draw your pretty towers in this frame.

Color me in.

Hot Air Balloon

This pretty petal print will make your hot air balloon look gorgeous.

Oval Pattern

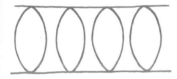

Draw two horizontal lines with oval shapes in between them.

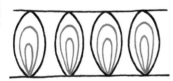

Add two teardrop shapes inside each oval.

Between each oval, draw a triangle with a short line inside it.

Practice the pattern here.

Decorative Designs

1. Start by drawing a teardrop with a flat bottom edge. Add a square shape for the basket with a long sausage shape along the top.

2. Draw curved lines across your balloon dividing it into sections. Divide the basket into sections as well.

3. Start to fill in the sections of the balloon, using the oval pattern, scalloped lines, and flower patterns.

4. Continue to fill in the sections of your balloon, using larger scalloped lines, petal shapes, and semicircle patterns.

5. Fill in any remaining blank spaces on your balloon with circles, dots, and teardrop shapes.

6. Decorate the basket with scalloped lines and draw small lines underneath. Finally, draw four long lines from the basket to the middle of the balloon to create the rope holding them together.

Draw your hot air balloon in this frame.

Color me in.